A Young Citizen's Guide to News Literacy

THE MEDIA'S ROLE IN DEMOCRACY

Jill Keppeler

PowerKiDS press

New York

Published in 2019 by The Rosen Publishing Group, Inc.
29 East 21st Street, New York, NY 10010

Copyright © 2019 by The Rosen Publishing Group, Inc.

All rights reserved. No part of this book may be reproduced in any form without permission in writing from the publisher, except by a reviewer.

First Edition

Editor: Jill Keppeler
Book Design: Reann Nye

Photo Credits: Cover Hero Images/Getty Images; p. 5 Oscar Wong/Moment/Getty Images; p. 6 https://commons.wikimedia.org/wiki/File:Betsy-Ross-Flag.jpg ; p. 7 https://commons.wikimedia.org/wiki/File:Boston_News-Letter_(first_issue).jpeg; pp. 9, 19 Bettmann/Getty Images; p. 10 https://commons.wikimedia.org/wiki/File:George_Mason_portrait.jpg; p. 11 https://commons.wikimedia.org/wiki/File:James_Madison.jpg; p. 13 Keystone/Hulton Archive/Getty Images; p. 15 Courtesy of the Library of Congress; p. 17 (left) https://commons.wikimedia.org/wiki/File:Ida_M_Tarbell_crop.jpg; P. 17 (right) Chicago History Museum/Archive Photos/Getty Images; pp. 21, 23 CBS Photo Archive/CBS/Getty Images; p. 24 https://en.wikipedia.org/wiki/File:Richard_M._Nixon,_ca._1935_-_1982_-_NARA_-_530679_(3x4).jpg; p. 25 The Washington Post/Getty Images; p. 26 https://commons.wikimedia.org/wiki/File:Challenger_explosion.jpg ; p. 27 Andrew Lichtenstein/Corbis Historical/Getty Images; p. 29 Willie B. Thomas/DigitalVision/Getty Images; p. 30 PeopleImages/E+/Getty Images.

Cataloging-in-Publishing Data

Names: Keppeler, Jill.
Title: The media's role in democracy / Jill Keppeler.
Description: New York : PowerKids Press, 2019. | Series: A young citizen's guide to news literacy | Includes glossary and index.
Identifiers: ISBN 9781538346167 (pbk.) | ISBN 9781538345023 (library bound) | ISBN 9781538346174 (6 pack)
Subjects: LCSH: Mass media–Political aspects–United States–Juvenile literature. | Press and politics–United States–Juvenile literature.
Classification: LCC P95.82.U6 K47 2019 | DDC 302.23'0973–dc23

Manufactured in the United States of America

CPSIA Compliance Information: Batch #CWPK19: For Further Information contact Rosen Publishing, New York, New York at 1-800-237-9932

CONTENTS

LIBERTY OF THE PRESS 4
IN THE COLONIES 6
REVOLUTIONARY WORDS 8
MAKE NO LAW 10
PARTISAN PAPERS AND POLITICS 12
GREATER INDEPENDENCE 14
YELLOW JOURNALISTS AND MUCKRAKERS 16
ON THE AIR 18
THE RISE OF TELEVISION 20
THE TELEVISION WAR 22
WATERGATE 24
24/7 26
ON THE WEB 28
THE QUEST CONTINUES 30
GLOSSARY 31
INDEX 32
WEBSITES 32

LIBERTY OF THE PRESS

What ideas and images do you associate with U.S. democracy? Do you think of the Founding Fathers meeting to create and approve the U.S. Constitution? Do you think of citizens gathering to vote for leaders and laws? Or do you think of the U.S. Capitol in Washington, D.C., and the people elected to represent us there?

None of these things would be possible without the open sharing of ideas and information. Forms of news media, including news websites, TV and radio broadcasts, magazines, and newspapers, spread this information and make it possible for U.S. citizens to educate themselves about issues and events so they can make good decisions. Since the earliest roots of U.S. democracy, the free press has had a key role, or part, in the great American experiment.

BREAKING NEWS

Article XVI of the state constitution of Massachusetts, created in 1780, states "The liberty of the press is essential [necessary] to the security of freedom in a state: it ought not, therefore, to be restrained in this commonwealth."

The word "media" can also refer to other forms of communication, including entertainment media such as movies and television shows. This book refers to the role of the news media.

DEMOCRACY OR REPUBLIC?

A democracy is a government run by the people, directly or indirectly. Most of the people of the United States don't directly run their government or make laws, but they do elect representatives to run it. This makes the U.S. government a representative democracy, which is also called a republic. It's also a constitutional democracy, which means a constitution limits the will of the majority to protect individual rights.

IN THE COLONIES

Newspapers were the first news media in the colonies that eventually formed the United States, but they weren't much like the newspapers we know today. Postmasters, who were in charge of the mail, and printers, who already had the equipment needed, started many colonial newspapers to make some extra money. Most papers were four pages long and full of very short items, many taken from other newspapers. There were no headlines and few pictures.

These earlier newspaper publishers had to be very careful. Each newspaper had to have a license from the government. Government officials could take it away quickly if they didn't like what the publishers printed—and send the publishers to jail! But as the colonists became more and more unhappy with British rule, newspapers spread the word.

BREAKING NEWS

There were 37 weekly newspapers in the 13 British colonies by the time the American Revolution began in 1775.

6

Boston postmaster and editor John Campbell published the first issue of the *Boston News-Letter* (shown here) on April 24, 1704.

THE FIRST NEWSPAPER

The first newspaper in the colonies, printed in 1690 in Boston, Massachusetts, was *Publick Occurrences, Both Foreign and Domestick*. The owners of this small paper didn't get the permission of the British government. They only printed one issue before the government shut it down, arrested the publisher, and destroyed all the copies. Fourteen years later, the *Boston News-Letter*—which was subsidized, or paid for, by the government—starting printing. It was the only newspaper in the colonies until 1719.

REVOLUTIONARY WORDS

By the middle of the 1700s, the press was speaking out about the colonists' discontent with the British government. For the first time, newspapers focused more on what was happening in the colonies than what was happening in Europe. As the government started directly taxing the colonists, newspapers reported on those taxes. And when tensions rose because of taxes, they reported on those, too. Most newspapers leaned toward colonial sympathies, but a few supported Great Britain.

As newspapers exchanged stories, colonists read the same things and banded together. Pamphlets promoted and shared by newspapers, such as *Common Sense* by Thomas Paine or *Letters from a Farmer in Pennsylvania*, shared revolutionary feelings. Via newspapers, a group of patriots led by Samuel Adams invited colonists to speak out against British policies. Many did so.

BREAKING NEWS

After the Founding Fathers approved the Declaration of Independence on July 4, 1776, the *Philadelphia Evening Post* published it on the front page two days later.

During the American Revolution from 1775 to 1783, newspapers kept Americans involved even when the fighting wasn't nearby. Battlefield news, however, was often late and somewhat confused.

Cornwallis TAKEN!

BOSTON, (Friday) October 26, 1781.

This Morning an Express arrived from Providence to HIS EXCELLENCY the GOVERNOR, with the following IMPORTANT INTELLIGENCE, viz.—

———

PROVIDENCE, Oct. 25, 1781. Three o'Clock, P.M.

This Moment an Express arrived at his Honor the Deputy-Governor's, from Col. Christopher Olney, Commandant on Rhode-Island, announcing the important Intelligence of the Surrender of Lord CORNWALLIS and his Army; an Account of which was Printed this Morning at Newport, and

JOHN PETER ZENGER

In 1734, John Peter Zenger, the publisher of the *New York Weekly Journal*, was arrested and charged with **libel** because of articles he'd printed that were critical of colonial Governor William Cosby. In a trial in 1735, Zenger's lawyer, Andrew Hamilton, argued that the jury should find Zenger not guilty because the articles were true. The jury did so, a milestone that later affected laws about the press in the United States.

MAKE NO LAW

As many of the young country's Founding Fathers came together to create the U.S. Constitution in 1787, many delegates wanted it to include a statement of rights for American citizens. After the states approved the Constitution, which went into effect in March 1789, leaders began **debating** the contents of this statement of rights.

In June 1789, James Madison, who later became the fourth president of the United States, proposed a list of constitutional amendments, including a provision for freedom of the press. After much debate, in December 1791, the states ratified, or approved, these first 10 amendments to the Constitution, which are called the Bill of Rights. The First Amendment includes the freedoms of speech and of the press.

BREAKING NEWS

George Mason of Virginia was a delegate at the Constitutional Convention. Before that, though, he'd written Virginia's Declaration of Rights, which also called for a free press. His words inspired the First Amendment.

At first, James Madison didn't think the United States needed a Bill of Rights. He thought the Constitution alone was enough. However, many other representatives thought a Bill of Rights was very important, so Madison proposed the amendments.

FAMOUS WORDS

The full text of the First Amendment to the U.S. Constitution is: "Congress shall make no law respecting an establishment of religion, or prohibiting [forbidding] the free exercise thereof; or abridging [taking away] the freedom of speech, or of the press; or the right of the people peaceably to assemble, and to petition [ask] the government for a redress [relief from] of grievances [issues]."

PARTISAN PAPERS AND POLITICS

By 1790, there were about 100 newspapers in the United States. The accepted standard of more **objective** news reporting didn't exist yet, however, and these papers tended to divide along the lines of the Federalist or Republican political parties, which openly **sponsored** them. Many politicians, including John Adams, the second president of the United States, disliked their criticism.

Adams introduced the **Sedition** Act in 1798, right as the United States was facing a possible war with France. This act made it illegal to publish false or **malicious** writing against the government or to **incite** opposition to any act of Congress or the president. It was used entirely against members of the press who opposed Adams or his Federalist Party before the Sedition Act ended in 1801.

Many presidents throughout history have been irritated by the news media. President Franklin D. Roosevelt, who held office from 1933 to 1945, once made a reporter sit in the corner! However, a reporter's job is to hold people in power **accountable**.

MUCH INFLAMED

While many of the Founding Fathers understood the importance of a free press, that didn't always mean they liked it—especially when it took aim at them. In 1783, George Washington told his troops that if the freedom of speech is taken away "dumb and silent we may be led, like sheep, to the slaughter." However, he also raged, in private, against a particular newspaper that kept criticizing him. "The president was much inflamed [enraged]," Thomas Jefferson noted later.

GREATER INDEPENDENCE

By the mid-1800s, newspapers were becoming more independent and less tied to political parties. They began reporting the news more often and reporters (now a true profession) actively went looking for news to report. As printing **technology** became more affordable, the number of newspapers grew and those newspapers became cheaper. By 1850, there were more than 2,500 newspapers in the United States.

While newspapers of this time weren't as tied to political parties, some did focus on certain issues. **Abolitionist** newspapers, such as the *North Star*, published by Frederick Douglass, and the *Liberator*, published by William Lloyd Garrison, called for the end of slavery. As the Civil War began in 1861, reporters followed the Union and Confederate armies, reporting on battles. Newspapers published lists of those killed or injured, an important service.

BREAKING NEWS

One role of news media is to expose readers to new ideas. Abolitionist newspapers gave some Americans a point of view they hadn't considered before. These papers spread the idea that slavery needed to be abolished.

Some people hated the idea that newspapers could spread an antislavery message. This 1835 drawing shows a proslavery mob burning abolitionist newspapers in Charleston, South Carolina.

YELLOW JOURNALISTS AND MUCKRAKERS

Toward the end of the 19th century, a competition for readers began between Joseph Pulitzer's *World* and William Randolph Hearst's *Journal* in New York City. Pulitzer aimed to print news he thought regular citizens would read. He focused on crime stories and exciting headlines, and Hearst followed. While these "yellow **journalism**" stories pulled in readers, they were often **sensationalized** and not completely true.

However, in the early part of the 20th century, a group of journalists called the muckrakers followed. Muckrakers such as Ida Tarbell and Upton Sinclair wrote newspaper and magazine articles and books. They called attention to many social issues in the United States, including social problems and political **corruption**, helping the Progressive Era reform movement and expanding the role of journalists as society's watchdogs.

BREAKING NEWS

Yellow journalism could be a kind of propaganda, which is when people spread ideas, information, or rumors for the purpose of helping or hurting someone or something.

Journalists Ida Tarbell, left, and Ida B. Wells were two muckrakers whose work made a difference in the United States. Tarbell wrote about unfair business practices and many other topics. Wells took on many issues that affected African Americans, including unfair voting laws.

ON THE AIR

In the 1920s, a new form of news media appeared to challenge newspapers. Broadcast radio became the first electronic mass medium, growing to about 30 stations in the United States by 1921. By 1922, more than 550 stations were on the air. By 1924, there were 1,400.

By the 1930s, radio was in its golden age. While it was often entertainment, it had a great effect on news as well. People could listen to live political events, such as the Democratic and Republican conventions, and hear leaders speak for themselves. During World War II, from 1939 to 1945, radio was the main source of news for Americans. Reporters broadcast from locations around the world. In addition to real news, however, the government often used radio for propaganda purposes.

BREAKING NEWS

A radio station in Detroit, Michigan, produced the first radio news broadcast (featuring election returns) on August 31, 1920. The *Detroit News* started radio station WWJ just in case the new medium overtook newspapers.

Some of the big names you can still see in broadcasting today got their start during the golden age of radio. The National Broadcasting Company (NBC) started in 1926, followed by the Columbia Broadcasting System (CBS) in 1927. In this photo, presidential candidate Herbert Hoover speaks during a 1928 NBC broadcast.

FIRESIDE CHATS

Political leaders quickly learned they could use radio to send messages directly to the public. President Franklin D. Roosevelt started his Fireside Chat broadcasts not long after he took office in 1933. In these, he explained the actions he was taking to deal with the Great Depression. While the broadcasts did provide information to the American people, they also gave Roosevelt a useful way to convey and promote his message without going through the press.

19

THE RISE OF TELEVISION

Even as radio blossomed as a news medium in the United States, another form of mass media was on the rise. CBS and NBC both started TV stations in 1941. By 1947, they'd formed TV networks, or systems, and the American Broadcasting Company (ABC) joined them a year later.

At first, news broadcasts simply included people reading the news while the station showed pictures or older video. As technology improved, so did the broadcasts. By 1951, news reports could be sent electronically throughout the country. Broadcasts switched to color film. News reports became longer. In 1961, TV networks first broadcast a presidential news conference live. The live news era had begun, and news would never be the same. By 1963, more people relied on television than newspapers for their news.

BREAKING NEWS

When President John F. Kennedy was assassinated, or killed, in 1963, TV stations were able to show live, breaking news about the tragedy for days.

In 1969, millions of people watched the astronauts of Apollo 11 on live television as the mission took off, landed on the moon, and returned safely to Earth.

THE POWER OF TRUTH

Edward R. Murrow started in radio, reporting during World War II, and eventually moved to television, producing the CBS news program *See It Now* and others. On the show in 1954, Murrow spoke out against U.S. Senator Joseph McCarthy, who used questionable means to accuse many Americans of being part of the Communist Party. McCarthy's accusations, often baseless, ruined many people's careers and lives. Using facts against the senator's own words, Murrow exposed McCarthy's lies, leading to the senator's downfall.

THE TELEVISION WAR

By the time the United States became involved in the Vietnam War in the mid-1960s, television news was in full swing. As U.S. troops poured into the conflict in 1965, the news media went, too. The Vietnam War became the first "television war," as reporters showed U.S. residents the realities of war from half a world away.

As time went on, although government reports said the war was going well, media reports sometimes showed otherwise. The public view of the war changed—not just due to the news reports but also due to the growing number of American deaths. In February 1968, trusted television journalist Walter Cronkite said (in an opinion piece) that the conflict was "mired in stalemate," or stuck in a draw. That was a tipping point in public opinion.

BREAKING NEWS

In 1968, more than 600 journalists from newspapers, magazines, radio stations, and TV stations were in Vietnam to cover the war. More than 60 journalists were killed during the conflict.

CBS journalist and anchorman Walter Cronkite visited Vietnam in 1968 to learn more after he became convinced the government wasn't telling the truth about the war. Responsible journalists are supposed to tell the truth, not what other people want them to say.

THE PENTAGON PAPERS

The news media continued to report on the circumstances of U.S. involvement in Vietnam. In 1971, the *New York Times* began to publish a series of articles based on the so-called Pentagon Papers, which contained a history of that involvement. The U.S. Department of Justice tried to stop the stories, but the *Times* and the *Washington Post* took the case to the U.S. Supreme Court and won the right to publish the information.

23

WATERGATE

In the early 1970s, a series of events brought new attention to the news media and journalists' role in reporting the truth. In June 1972, police arrested five people in an apparent burglary at the Democratic National Committee headquarters at the Watergate office complex, or buildings, in Washington, D.C. This was very minor news at the time.

However, two young reporters at the *Washington Post*, Carl Bernstein and Bob Woodward, kept reporting and digging and eventually broke a number of stories linked to that first burglary. These stories showed wrongdoing on the part of members of the Nixon reelection campaign and a cover-up by White House staff and the president himself. These stories, along with investigations by the government, led to Nixon's resignation in August 1974.

Richard Nixon

Throughout the investigations into the Watergate break-in, Nixon and his White House staff denied any wrongdoing and accused the reporters of lying. This is why reporters such as Woodward, left, and Bernstein must be determined.

25

24/7

Sources of news kept changing and adapting to new technology. In the latter half of the 20th century, cable TV (in which TV signals are transmitted by cable to homes) rose in popularity and availability. The amount of TV networks available to more people expanded from "the big three" of NBC, CBS, and ABC to countless stations. More than half of homes in the United States had cable by 1990.

The first 24-hour news network was Cable News Network (CNN) in 1980. The network struggled for viewers at first, but after it provided live coverage of the space shuttle *Challenger* explosion in 1986 and then constant coverage of the Persian Gulf War in 1991, viewers became accustomed to the flow of information. In fact, they began to expect it.

BREAKING NEWS

CNN was followed by more news networks, including MSNBC, CNBC, and Fox News. Each has its own shows and focus.

As the 21st century started, news sources had to cover one of the biggest news stories since television coverage began. The September 11, 2001, attacks on New York City led to hours of coverage as journalists and other citizens alike struggled to deal with what had happened.

DOWNFALL?

Because cable news stations have so much time to fill, they often have shows filled with analysis, or close study, of the news. Sometimes they focus more on very dramatic stories. And sometimes they add more opinion, which classic journalism avoids (except in rare and clearly labeled cases) in favor of objective news reporting. Because of this, some think American journalism fell in quality as these networks grew.

ON THE WEB

As the World Wide Web took off in the 1990s and the number of home computers grew, more people started getting their news online. Newspapers, magazines, and TV stations created websites to deliver the news. In 1986, only 12 percent of U.S. adults got some of their news from online sources. By 2016, 81 percent did.

Soon, people created online news sources that didn't have a print or broadcast product at all. This put even more information out there—but sometimes without the standards traditional journalists often followed. Anyone could (and can) post anything online and make it look like a real story. This problem continues today with the issue of "fake news." Like in the days of yellow journalism, some so-called news sources aim more at gaining readers or viewers than publishing the truth and fairness.

BREAKING NEWS

The first newspaper to go online was the *Columbus Dispatch* on July 1, 1980. It was part of an experiment with the Associated Press and CompuServe Internet service.

Fake news stories online rose during the 2016 U.S. presidential campaign. Many people shared these stories over social media.

SOCIAL MEDIA SIGNS

As social media sites such as Facebook and Twitter became popular, more people started getting news from posts there. Many posts, however, aren't reliable. Does the post link back to an established news source and have the name of the reporter? This is a good sign. Is the post trying to sell you something? Is it trying to make you mad? These aren't good signs. See if you can find the basic facts elsewhere before you share.

THE QUEST CONTINUES

As technology and journalism continue to grow and change, the quest for truth—for both good news reporters and smart news consumers—continues. News consumers must be careful to make sure what they're reading is real before using that information to make decisions, including who they believe and who they vote for.

A democracy still needs educated, informed citizens to remain healthy. Citizens must seek out the truth and news sources must provide it—even if some people don't want them to do so. The Founding Fathers protected freedom of speech and freedom of the press in part because they remembered how leaders in Great Britain limited news they didn't like. Even as forms of news media grow and change, these freedoms (and responsibilities) are just as important today.

Whatever form of news you read, listen to, or watch, it's good to stay informed!

GLOSSARY

abolitionist: Someone who wants to abolish, or end, slavery.

accountable: Required to be responsible for something.

corruption: Illegal or dishonest behavior, especially by people in power.

debate: To argue or discuss something.

incite: To cause someone to act in a harmful way.

journalism: The collecting, writing, and editing of news stories for newspapers, magazines, websites, television, or radio.

libel: A false statement about someone that hurts their reputation.

malicious: With a desire to cause harm to someone or something.

objective: Not influenced by personal feelings; based on facts.

sedition: The act of doing something that encourages people to disobey their government.

sensationalize: To make something more shocking than it already is.

sponsor: To pay for or plan and carry out a project or activity.

technology: A method that uses science to solve problems and the tools used to solve those problems.

INDEX

A
American Revolution, 6, 8, 9

B
Bernstein, Carl, 24, 25
Bill of Rights, 10, 11

C
Civil War, 14
Cronkite, Walter, 22, 23

D
Declaration of Independence, 8

F
fake news, 28, 29
Founding Fathers, 4, 8, 10, 13, 30

M
Madison, James, 10, 11
muckrakers, 16, 17
Murrow, Edward R., 21

P
propaganda, 16, 18
Pulitzer, Joseph, 16

S
social media, 29

U
U.S. Constitution, 4, 10, 11

V
Vietnam War, 22, 23

W
Woodward, Bob, 24, 25

Y
yellow journalism, 16, 28

Z
Zenger, John Peter, 9

WEBSITES

Due to the changing nature of Internet links, PowerKids Press has developed an online list of websites related to the subject of this book. This site is updated regularly. Please use this link to access the list: www.powerkidslinks.com/newslit/democracy